MICHAEL AVERY

Spark to Park: Making the Most of Your Electric Vehicle Experience

Insights and Pro Tips for Seamless EV Maintenance

Contents

1

Introduction

Welcome to "Spark to Park: Making the Most of Your Electric Vehicle Experience; Key Insights and Pro Tips for Seamless EV Maintenance," a comprehensive guide designed to enhance your journey into the dynamic world of electric vehicles (EVs).

The dawn of electric vehicles marks a revolutionary shift in how we perceive and engage with personal transportation. This book is crafted for both the enthusiastic newcomer and the seasoned EV driver, aiming to demystify the nuances of electric vehicle ownership, maintenance, and optimization. As we stand on the brink of a sustainable revolution, the switch from gasoline to electricity isn't just a change in energy sources—it's a transformation in our lifestyle, attitudes, and the very rhythm of our daily travels.

As you turn these pages, you'll dive into a pool of essential knowledge covering the intricate workings of EVs, the secrets to maximizing their lifespan and efficiency, and the nuts and bolts of routine maintenance. We'll embark on a journey that starts with the very spark—an overview of electric vehicle technology—and ends in the park, where your EV rests, efficiently charged and ready for your next adventure.

This book is more than just a manual; it's a companion in your transition to exploring electric vehicles. It's divided into digestible sections, each packed with practical tips, expert advice, and insights from years of research and real-world experience. We will explore:

Understanding Your EV: Delving into the heart of electric vehicles, from their motors to their batteries, and how they differ fundamentally from traditional internal combustion engine vehicles.

Charging Smart: Unraveling the mysteries of EV charging, including types of chargers, charging speeds, and how to set up your home for efficient charging.

Maintenance Musts: Outlining the critical maintenance tasks specific to EVs, debunking myths, and providing a routine to keep your vehicle in top shape.

Maximizing Range and Efficiency: Techniques and habits to extend your battery life and maximize mileage, ensuring your EV is as cost-effective as it is environmentally friendly.

Navigating the EV Ecosystem: Understanding the broader EV ecosystem, including incentives, regulations, and the evolving landscape of electric mobility.

Troubleshooting and Tips: Offering solutions to common issues and sharing pro tips to enhance your EV experience.

Whether you're contemplating the purchase of your first electric vehicle or looking to deepen your understanding and aptitude with your current EV, "Spark to Park" promises to be an invaluable resource. Our journey together will empower you with the knowledge and confidence to embrace the exciting, sustainable, and ever-evolving world of electric vehicles.

So, buckle up, and let's embark on this electrifying journey together!

2

Chapter 1: Understanding Your Electric Vehicle

Essential Components of an EV

Battery

At the heart of every electric vehicle (EV) lies the battery, a critical component that stores the electrical energy needed to power the EV. Unlike conventional gasoline cars, where performance is gauged by engine displacement or horsepower, an EV's prowess is significantly defined by its battery capacity, typically measured in kilowatt-hours (kWh). This capacity isn't just a number — it directly impacts your EV's range and efficiency. The rule of thumb is straightforward: larger batteries equate to longer ranges, enabling you to travel further on a single charge. However, this comes with trade-offs in increased cost and weight, which can affect the vehicle's dynamics and charging time.

Electric Motor

Transitioning from the battery to the electric motor of an EV is a marvel of modern engineering. In stark contrast to the noisy, vibration-heavy internal combustion engines of gasoline vehicles, electric motors are silent, smooth operators. They convert electrical energy into mechanical energy, powering the wheels. A notable advantage of electric motors is their ability to deliver immediate torque, which simply means that the acceleration in an EV is not just quick — it's instant, offering a dynamic and responsive driving experience.

Inverter

Another unsung hero within your EV is the inverter. This component might seem enigmatic, but its role is pivotal. It converts the direct current (DC) from your EV's battery into alternating current (AC), electricity that powers the motor. The efficiency of this conversion process greatly influences your EV's performance, dictating how effectively and smoothly the vehicle translates battery power into motion.

Charging System

Let's talk about powering up your EV, a process as crucial as refueling a gasoline car but with its own nuances. The charging system comprises several elements — the on-board charger, the plug, and the charging cable. Charging systems can range widely, from Level 1 chargers, your standard 120V household outlets, offering the convenience of home charging but with slower speeds, to Level 3 or DC fast chargers. These high-voltage chargers are game-changers, capable of charging your EV's battery to about 80% in as little as 30 minutes. However, it's worth noting that frequent use of fast charging can impact the long-term health of your battery.

Understanding Charging Levels

For a first-time EV owner, understanding the different levels of charging is essential:

- **Level 1 Charging:** This is the most accessible form of charging, using a standard 120V outlet. It's perfect for overnight charging or topping up your EV at home, though it's the slowest charging method, often delivering about 4-6 miles of range per hour of charging.

- **Level 2 Charging:** Upgrading to Level 2, you're looking at 240V, similar to what large appliances in your home use. These chargers can significantly speed up your charging time, delivering about 10-60 miles of range per hour. They are often found in public charging stations and can be installed at home.

- **Level 3 Charging / DC Fast Charging**: This is where charging gets swift. DC fast chargers are typically in public charging stations along highways or urban centers. They are ideal for long-distance travel, providing rapid charging speeds that can be game-changers during a road trip.

How EVs Differ from Gasoline-Powered Vehicles

In essence, EVs represent a paradigm shift in automotive technology. Besides the obvious differences in fuel source (electricity vs. gasoline), EVs boast fewer moving parts, potentially lowering maintenance needs and costs. The absence of an exhaust system, oil changes, and a simpler, more robust power train are just a few benefits that set EVs apart.

Benefits of Owning an EV

Environmental Impact: By driving an EV, you're contributing to reduced air pollution and greenhouse gas emissions. EVs, especially when charged from renewable energy sources, represent a cleaner mode of transportation.

Lower Maintenance Needs: With fewer moving parts and fluids to change, EVs typically have lower ongoing maintenance needs than gasoline-powered vehicles.

Performance: The performance of an EV is not to be underestimated. The quiet but swift acceleration, the low center of gravity due to battery placement, and the generally higher torque make EVs fun to drive.

As a first-time EV owner, embarking on this electric journey can feel like stepping into a new world. With these fundamentals in hand, you are well-equipped to understand the groundbreaking technology you're now in command of. Welcome to the future of driving!

Chapter 2: Regular Maintenance Checks

Maintaining your electric vehicle (EV) is vital for ensuring its longevity, efficiency, and safety. Unlike gasoline cars, EVs have different maintenance needs, primarily focused on the battery, tires, braking system, and software. Here's a more detailed guide for first-time EV owners on how to keep their vehicles in top condition:

Battery Care

Monitoring Battery Health

The battery is not just the power source but the most expensive component in your EV.

To monitor its health:

- Avoid Extreme Temperatures: Long exposures to very high or low temperatures can degrade your battery faster.

Parking in shaded areas or using a garage can help mitigate temperature extremes.

- Optimal Charging Range: Keep your battery's charge between 20% and 80%. Consistently charging it to full or running it to zero can shorten its lifespan.

Tips for Maximizing Battery Life

Charging Habits: Frequent rapid (Level 3) charging can stress your battery. Where possible, use Level 1 or Level 2 charging.

- Charging Habits: Frequent rapid (Level 3) charging can stress your battery. Where possible, use Level 1 or Level 2 charging.
- Smart Charging: Some EVs have smart charging features that allow you to set charging schedules or limits to protect battery health.

Tire Maintenance

Regular Checks for Wear and Pressure

Tires play a critical role in your EV's performance and efficiency. Regular checks every month and before long trips are advised. Keep an eye out for:

Tire Pressure: Under- or over-inflated tires can affect your EV's range, handling, and safety. Check the pressure against the manufacturer's recommendation.

Wear and Tear: Look for uneven wear patterns, which might indicate alignment or suspension issues.

Impact of Tires on Range and Performance: Low Rolling Resistance Tires are designed to improve range and efficiency in EVs. They reduce the energy lost due to tire deformation during motion.

Braking System

Regenerative Braking and Its Advantages
   Regenerative braking is a distinctive feature of EVs, where the electric motor helps slow the vehicle, converting kinetic energy back into stored energy in the battery. This system:

Extends Brake Life: By using the motor to decelerate, the physical brake pads and discs endure less wear and tear.

Improves Efficiency: It can increase your overall driving range and efficiency.

When to Check Brake Pads and Discs: Regular brake inspections are recommended every 10,000 to 20,000 miles, but this can vary based on driving habits and conditions. Look out for any unusual noises, feelings, or responsiveness during braking.

Cooling System

An EV's cooling system ensures the battery and motor operate within their optimal temperature range. This system is vital for preventing overheating, which can permanently reduce battery capacity and motor performance. Regular checks should include:

Coolant Levels: Ensure the coolant level is within the recommended range.

System Integrity: Check for any leaks or damages in the cooling system.

Regular Maintenance Checks

While EVs generally require less maintenance than gasoline cars, following the manufacturer's maintenance schedule is vital. These checks often focus on:

Software Updates: Like your smartphone, your EV's software needs updates. These can improve vehicle performance, range, and functionality.

Battery and Electrical Systems: Professional checks on the battery pack and electrical systems can preemptively spot issues.

By being proactive and informed about these maintenance aspects, you can not only enhance your EV's performance and lifespan but also enjoy a safer, more efficient driving experience. As a first-time EV owner, embracing these new routines will ensure you are part of a cleaner, more sustainable driving future.

Chapter 3: Charging Your EV

For new EV owners, understanding how to charge their vehicles efficiently and effectively is crucial. This chapter will guide you through the different types of charging, how to charge your EV at home, using public charging stations, and practices to maximize your battery's life.

Types of Charging: Slow, Fast, and Rapid

Slow Charging (Level 1)

Source: Standard 120V household outlet.

Charging Time: 8 to 20 hours to charge fully, depending on your EV's battery.

Best For: Overnight charging or topping up at work.

Fast Charging (Level 2)

Source: 240V outlet (similar to what's used for heavy appliances like dryers).

Charging Time: Typically, 4 to 6 hours for a full charge.

Best For: Daily use, offering a practical balance between speed and battery care.

Rapid Charging (DC Fast Chargers)
Source: Specialized public charging stations.
Charging Time: Around 30 minutes to get to 80% charge.
Best For: Long trips where time is of the essence.

How to Charge Your EV at Home

Installation: It's advisable to have a certified electrician install a Level 2 charging station at your home.

Benefits: Faster than Level 1, convenient, and can be scheduled during off-peak electricity hours to save on costs.

Smart Charging: Many home chargers have smart features allowing remote control and monitoring of charging sessions.

Public Charging Stations: What to Know

Location: Widely available at shopping centers, parking lots, and dedicated EV charging stations.

Charging Network Membership: Some networks offer subscription plans for better rates.

Payment and Access: This can vary from free stations to pay-per-use. Some require specific network membership cards or apps.

Etiquette: Remember to unplug and move your EV once charged, making room for other users.

Maximizing Battery Life through Optimal Charging Practices

Routine: Frequent, smaller charges (keeping the battery between 20% and 80%) can be more beneficial than waiting for the battery to almost empty.

Temperature Considerations: Extreme temperatures can affect charging speed and battery health. Some EVs have thermal management systems to mitigate this.

Software Updates: Ensure your EV's software is up-to-date, as manufacturers often release updates that improve charging efficiency and battery management.

For first-time EV owners, mastering these charging practices not only ensures your vehicle is always ready to go but also plays a pivotal role in maintaining your battery's health over its lifespan. Familiarizing yourself with your EV's specific charging requirements and the infrastructure around you can significantly enhance your EV experience, ensuring convenience and reliability in your everyday travel.

Chapter 4: Understanding Range and Efficiency

The ability of an electric vehicle (EV) to travel long distances on a single charge and its efficiency in using stored energy are two crucial considerations for EV owners. For first-time EV owners, understanding the nuances of range and efficiency can be empowering, allowing you to make the most out of every charge and optimize your driving experience.

Factors Affecting EV Range

Driving Habits

Like gasoline vehicles, your driving style dramatically affects your EV's consumption rate. Smooth acceleration, controlled braking, and steady speeds can considerably increase your range.

Terrain and Climate

Driving uphill or on mountainous terrains consumes more

power. Furthermore, extreme temperatures, either hot or cold, can strain the battery. Using the vehicle's heater in winter or air conditioner in summer can also deplete the battery faster.

Vehicle Load and Auxiliary Systems

Apart from heavy loads or towing, even using in-car systems like entertainment, navigation, or heated seats can draw significant power. Remember, every accessory or feature in use will impact the battery life.

Tips to Maximize Range

Eco Modes

Many EVs come with driving modes that prioritize efficiency. Engaging such modes can optimize various vehicle systems for maximum range.

Regenerative Braking

Use your EV's regenerative braking feature, which captures and converts some of the energy typically lost during braking back into stored power.

Stay Updated

Regular software updates offer improvements in battery management and efficiency. Keeping your vehicle's software updated can lead to better range and performance.

Plan Ahead

If you're going on a longer journey, planning your route to avoid steep terrains and using apps that locate charging stations can ensure you always have enough charge.

How to Read and Understand Efficiency Metrics

Efficiency Metrics

While the metric kWh/100 miles is commonly used, some regions or vehicles might use miles/kWh. The latter measures how far your vehicle can travel on a single kilowatt-hour of electricity. Higher miles/kWh indicate better efficiency.

Compared to Gasoline Vehicles

Consider these metrics the inverse of a gasoline car's miles per gallon (mpg). In the EV world, consuming less energy (fewer kWh) to travel a certain distance is the goal.

Monitor and Adapt

Many EVs offer detailed breakdowns of energy consumption, providing insights into how different systems or driving behaviors affect efficiency. By monitoring this regularly, you can adapt to enhance your range and efficiency.

Transforming to an EV requires a slightly altered mindset. By understanding and adapting to factors that affect range and efficiency, first-time EV owners can optimize their driving habits, ensuring they get the best out of their new electric vehicle.

Chapter 5: Decoding the EV Dashboard and Features

Introduction to the EV Dashboard

Unlike traditional vehicles, an EV dashboard provides insights into battery health, range, and consumption patterns. Familiarizing yourself with these can significantly enhance your EV experience.

State of Charge

Similar to the fuel gauge in gasoline vehicles, the state of charge indicates how much battery power remains.

Energy Flow

Many EVs offer real-time visuals on energy consumption, showing power flow between the battery, motor, and other systems.

Regenerative Braking Indicator

This feature indicates when energy is being recovered during braking and fed back into the battery.

Advanced Features for Modern EVs

Adaptive Range Prediction

Using AI and machine learning, some advanced EVs can predict range based on driving habits, route topography, and other factors, offering a more accurate estimate than static range counters.

Remote Monitoring and Controls

Many EVs come equipped with smartphone apps allowing you to monitor the charging status, control climate settings, and even preheat or cool the vehicle remotely.

Chapter 6: Software Updates and Diagnostics

Importance of Software Updates in EVs

Software updates in EVs can enhance various aspects of the vehicle, including battery management, driving dynamics, and infotainment systems. Some updates can even unlock additional features or improve range and efficiency. Keeping your EV's software up to date ensures you're leveraging the latest improvements and bug fixes.

How to Update Your EV's Software

Most modern EVs offer over-the-air (OTA) updates, which can be downloaded and installed wirelessly. These updates can often be scheduled to occur during off-peak hours. It's essential to ensure your vehicle is connected to a Wi-Fi network to receive and install these updates seamlessly.

Understanding Diagnostic Alerts and What to Do

EVs are equipped with advanced diagnostics that monitor the vehicle's health, providing alerts for issues ranging from battery health to maintenance needs. Understanding these alerts, typically available through the vehicle's dashboard or associated app, is crucial. Responding promptly to maintenance and service alerts can prevent minor issues from becoming major and help maintain your EV's longevity and reliability.

Chapter 7: When to Seek Professional Maintenance

Every vehicle has nuances, and electric vehicles (EVs) are no exception. While they might require less frequent maintenance than traditional gasoline-powered cars, there are moments when a professional's expertise is essential.

Signs that your EV Needs Professional Attention

- **Warning Lights:** If any unfamiliar lights illuminate your dashboard, it's crucial to get them inspected, especially if they pertain to the battery or electric motor.

- **Reduction in Range:** If you notice a significant reduction in the expected range, it might indicate battery issues or other efficiency-reducing problems.

- **Unusual Noises:** While EVs are generally quieter, any unfamiliar sounds, especially from the motor or wheels, should be investigated.

- **Charging Issues:** Inconsistent charging or a complete failure to charge warrants a professional's attention.

- **Regenerative Braking Malfunctions:** If you observe your EV isn't recovering as much energy from braking as before, it might indicate a problem with the regenerative braking system.

Finding a Qualified EV Mechanic

With the rise of EVs, many mechanics specialize in electric vehicle care. When seeking one, ensure they are certified for your specific brand and model. Recommendations from fellow EV owners or online communities can also be a reliable way to find a trustworthy mechanic.

Warranty and Service Plans: What You Need to Know

Most EVs come with a warranty, especially for the battery. Always be familiar with the terms. Some issues might be covered, saving you out-of-pocket expenses. Additionally, consider extended warranties or service plans for peace of mind, but always read the fine print to ensure they offer value for money.

Chapter 8: Long-term EV Care

The longevity of your EV doesn't only hinge on regular maintenance but also on how you care for it over the years.

Preparing your EV for Long-term Storage

If you plan not to use your EV for an extended period:

- **Charge the Battery:** Store your vehicle with the battery charged between 50-80%.
- **Tire Care:** Inflate tires to the recommended pressure to avoid flat spots.
- **Clean Your EV:** Ensure it's free from dirt or contaminants.
- **Disconnect & Store:** If possible, disconnect the 12V auxiliary battery to prevent drainage.

Battery Longevity: Long-term Perspectives

An EV's battery might degrade over time. However, with care, you can prolong its life:

- Avoid regular deep discharges.
- Try to keep your battery charge between 20-80%.
- Minimize exposure to extreme temperatures.

Tips for Maintaining Value and Performance Over Time

- **Regular Software Updates:** Always update your EV's software, which can improve efficiency and even increase range.

- **Protect from Elements:** Use a car cover or park in a shaded area to protect the paint and battery.
- **Regular Health Checks:** Apart from regular maintenance, periodic deep inspections can help identify potential long-term issues.

Chapter 9: The Environmental and Economic Impact of EVs

Reducing Carbon Footprint

Electric vehicles play a pivotal role in reducing greenhouse gas emissions. With zero tailpipe emissions, they contribute to cleaner air and a reduction in urban noise pollution.

Lifecycle Emissions

It's essential to consider the entire lifecycle of the vehicle, from manufacturing to disposal. While EVs have a carbon footprint during production, especially the batteries, their overall emissions, considering their lifespan, are significantly lower than conventional vehicles.

Economic Benefits

Cost Savings: Although the upfront cost of EVs might be higher, the low operating costs, including savings on fuel and reduced maintenance, can offset this over time.

Government Incentives

Many governments offer incentives for purchasing EVs, such as tax credits, rebates, or reduced registration fees.

Chapter 10: EV Safety and Emergency Handling

Safety is a paramount concern in any vehicle, and EVs are no exception. Knowing how to handle your EV in emergencies and understanding its safety features are critical components of responsible EV ownership.

Emergency Protocols

In Case of Accidents

Know where the emergency disconnects are located in your EV. These switches allow you to disconnect the battery in emergencies, a crucial step in ensuring safety.

Handling Battery Fires

While rare, EV battery fires require different handling than typical car fires. It's essential to be aware of this and inform emergency services immediately if you suspect a battery fire.

Safety Features

Enhanced Safety Standards

EVs are subject to stringent safety testing and often come with advanced safety features due to the high voltage of their systems.

Driving Assistance Technologies

Many EVs come equipped with advanced driver-assistance systems (ADAS), such as automatic emergency braking, collision avoidance systems, and adaptive cruise control, enhancing overall safety.

Chapter 11: Navigating the U.S. Charging Network and Planning Your EV Trip

The United States has witnessed a rapid expansion in its electric vehicle (EV) charging infrastructure, making cross-country travel in an EV not just a possibility but a pleasant experience. For first-time EV owners, understanding this network and planning trips can seem daunting, but with the right tools and knowledge, it becomes a breeze. Here's a comprehensive guide to help you on your way.

Overview of the U.S. Charging Network

Types of Chargers

- **Level 1 (Slow Chargers):** These use a regular 120V AC outlet and are ideal for overnight charging at home.

- **Level 2 (Fast Chargers):** Operating at 240V AC, they can charge an EV within a few hours. These are commonly found at public charging stations, workplaces, and many homes.

- **DC Fast Chargers:** As the name suggests, these are the fastest chargers available, offering an 80% charge in under an hour. They're perfect for long-distance travel.

Major Charging Networks

Several companies operate extensive charging networks across the U.S. Some of the major ones include:

- **Tesla Supercharger Network:** Exclusively for Tesla vehicles, these fast-charging stations are strategically placed to facilitate long-distance travel.

- **Electrify America:** Born from the Volkswagen emissions scandal, this network is rapidly expanding, offering fast chargers compatible with most EVs.

- **ChargePoint:** One of the largest networks, they offer Level 2 and DC fast chargers.

- **EVgo:** EVgo's charging stations **focus** on fast charging and are typically found in urban areas and along major highways.

Planning Your EV Trip

Use Dedicated EV Navigation Tools

Many EVs have built-in navigation systems that factor in charging stops based on your vehicle's range and charger locations. Additionally, apps like PlugShare or A Better Route Planner allow you to plan trips, showing charger locations, types, and even user reviews about the charging stations.

Factor in Charging Time

Remember, charging is a more extended process than refueling a gasoline vehicle. Factor in the time you'll spend charging, and use it as an opportunity to rest, eat, or explore the local area.

Check Charger Compatibility

Ensure that the charging stations along your route are compatible with your vehicle. While many modern chargers are universal, some older models or specific brands (like Tesla) may require adapters.

Reserve Charging Spots

Some networks or locations allow you to reserve charging spots in advance, ensuring you don't have to wait.

Stay Updated on Your Vehicle's Charge Status

Modern EVs and charging networks offer smartphone integration, letting you monitor your vehicle's charging status and receive notifications when charging is complete.

Consider Backup Options

Always have a backup charging location in mind, especially in areas with sparse charging infrastructure. Having portable charging equipment for emergencies is also a smart move.

Embracing the Journey

Traveling with an EV offers a unique experience. The growing charging infrastructure in the U.S. not only makes EV travel feasible but also encourages exploration of lesser-known destinations, often found near charging stations. With some planning and an adventurous spirit, your EV journey can be as much about the ride as the destination.

Remember, the journey in an EV is not just about reaching from point A to B; it's about embracing a sustainable future, enjoying the serene silence of an electric drive, and being part of a community that's driving change, one charge at a time.

13

Conclusion: Embracing the Future on Four Wheels

As you turn the pages of this guide, one thing becomes crystal clear: owning an electric vehicle (EV) is much more than a simple shift in transportation — it's a vibrant journey into a future that is cleaner, quieter, and more harmonious with the earth.

For the first-time EV owner, you've embarked on a path less traveled, a road that whispers of innovation and an exciting challenge: to redefine what it means to drive and care for a vehicle. Owning an EV isn't just about replacing fuel with electricity; it's about being part of a movement that sees beyond the horizon.

A Vision of Sustainability: Every time you drive your EV, you contribute to a greener world. Your choice helps cut down on air pollution, reduce dependency on fossil fuels, and demonstrates a commitment to a sustainable lifestyle. The hum of the electric motor becomes more than just a sound — it's a resonating echo of your dedication to environmental stewardship.

Forward-Looking Technology: Electric vehicles are at the forefront of automotive technological advancements. From regenerative braking systems to cutting-edge battery technologies, your EV is a marvel of modern engineering. It offers a unique opportunity to engage with technology that is constantly evolving, promising an ever-improving driving experience.

Kindness to Our Planet and Wallets: Beyond the ecological impact, EVs offer a gentler footprint on your finances in the long run. Lower maintenance costs, government incentives, and freedom from fluctuating fuel prices mean that your investment in an EV extends its benefits beyond just environmental kindness. It's a prudent choice for both our planet and your pocket.

A Community of Pioneers: When you choose to drive an EV, you join a growing community of pioneers who are shaping the future of mobility. This community isn't just about sharing tips on vehicle maintenance or the best charging stations; it's a collective of forward-thinking individuals who share a vision and passion for a better world. Engage with this community through forums, social media, and local meet-ups to exchange stories, advice, and experiences.

The Joy of the Drive: Finally, remember the sheer joy of driving an EV. The immediate torque, the smooth acceleration, and the quiet ride are experiences that often turn EV skeptics into enthusiasts. Your journey in an EV is not just about reaching a destination; it's about enjoying every silent, swift moment on the road.

As you embark on this exhilarating journey with your new EV, remember that you're not just driving a vehicle; you're steering a part of the revolution. A revolution that is as much about cherishing our planet as it is about cherishing the journey itself. Welcome to a world where every mile matters, and every small step towards electric mobility paves the way for a cleaner, brighter future for future generations.

Welcome to the exhilarating world of electric vehicles!

14

Appendix: Additional Resources

Links to EV Maintenance Forums and Communities:

https://www.speakev.com/forums/
https://www.diyelectriccar.com/
https://www.insideevsforum.com/
https://electricvehicleforums.com/

Major Charging Networks in the US:

Electrify America
Tesla Supercharger Network
EVgo
Chargepoint

Resources:

Aa. (2021, July 1). *How to maintain and repair electric vehicles.* The AA. https://www.theaa.com/driving-advice/electric-vehicles/electric-car-maintenance#maintenance

Alternative Fuels Data Center: Developing infrastructure to charge electric vehicles. (n.d.). https://afdc.energy.gov/fuels/electricity_infrastructure.html

Capparella, J. (2022, August 8). Electric Cars vs. Gas Cars: Everything You Need to Know. *Car And Driver.* https://www.caranddriver.com/research/a32781943/electric-cars-vs-gas-cars/

Charger types and speeds. (n.d.). US Department of Transportation. https://www.transportation.gov/rural/ev/toolkit/ev-basics/charging-speeds

Electric cars, hybrids, and beyond | GreenCars. (n.d.). GreenCars. https://www.greencars.com/

Spendiff-Smith, M. (2023, June 21). *Levels of EV charging.* Power Sonic. https://www.power-sonic.com/blog/levels-of-ev-charging/

Understanding The Range & Efficiency Of Electric Vehicles | Recharged. (n.d.). https://www.recharged.com/understanding-range-and-efficiency